BOUNDLESS LOVE

CELEBRATING THE
ETERNAL SPIRIT
OF
MOTHERHOOD

LIN MOON

Boundless Love: Celebrating the Eternal Spirit of Motherhood

A Collection of Quotations About Motherhood

Lin Moon

Dedication

I DEDICATE THIS BOOK TO MY MOTHER, MARY KEENEN, WHO WAS LOVED BEYOND MEASURE

"To the world, you are a mother. But to your family, you are the world." - Unknown

"A mother's love is the fuel that enables a normal human being to do the impossible." - Marion C. Garretty

"Motherhood: All love begins and ends there."
- Robert Browning

"The influence of a mother in the lives of her children is beyond calculation." - James E. Faust

"A mother's arms
are more
comforting than
anyone else's." -
Princess Diana

"Mothers hold their children's hands for a short while, but their hearts forever." - Unknown

"Motherhood is the greatest thing and the hardest thing."
- Ricki Lake

"The love of a mother is the veil of a softer light between the heart and the heavenly Father." - Samuel Taylor Coleridge

"A mother's love is the purest love there is." - Unknown

"A mother is she who can take the place of all others but whose place no one else can take." - Cardinal Meymillod

"A mother's love is like a beacon, guiding us through the stormy seas of life." - Unknown

"Motherhood is the exquisite inconvenience of being another person's everything." - Unknown

"Motherhood is the biggest gamble in the world. It is the glorious life force. It's huge and scary - it's an act of infinite optimism." - Gilda Radner

"A mother's love is the heart of a home." - Unknown

"Motherhood is the greatest thing in the world when the right woman meets it." - Gloria Swanson

"Motherhood is the greatest gift and the greatest challenge." - Katherine Maslen

"A mother is not a person to lean on but a person to make leaning unnecessary." - Dorothy Canfield Fisher

"A mother's love is the key that opens the heart of a child." - Unknown

"Motherhood is the art
of raising a soul." -
Unknown

"Being a mother means that your heart is no longer yours; it wanders wherever your children go." - Unknown

"A mother's love for her child is like nothing else in the world. It knows no law, no pity, it dates all things and crushes down remorselessly all that stands in its path." - Agatha Christie

"A mother's love is patient and forgiving when all others are forsaking, it never fails or falters, even though the heart is breaking." - Helen Rice

"A mother's arms are made of tenderness and children sleep soundly in them." - Victor Hugo

"Motherhood is a choice you make every day, to put someone else's happiness and well-being ahead of your own, to teach the hard lessons, to do the right thing even when you're not sure what the right thing is... and to forgive yourself, over and over again, for doing everything wrong." - Donna Ball

"Mothers are like glue. Even when you can't see them, they're still holding the family together." - Susan Gale

"Motherhood has a very humanizing effect. Everything gets reduced to essentials." - Meryl Streep

"Mother's love is peace. It need not be acquired, it need not be deserved." - Erich Fromm

"The influence of a mother in the lives of her children is beyond calculation." - James E. Faust

"A mother's happiness is like a beacon, lighting up the future but reflected also on the past in the guise of fond memories." - Honore de Balzac

"The art of mothering is to teach the art of living to children." - Elaine Heffner

"The loveliest masterpiece of the heart of God is the heart of a mother." - St. Therese of Lisieux

"A mother understands what a child does not say." - Jewish Proverb

"Only mothers can think of the future because they give birth to it in their children." - Maxim Gorky

"To describe my mother would be to write about a hurricane in its perfect power." - Maya Angelou

"The best place to cry is on a mother's arms." - Jodi Picoult

"A mother's love is the fuel that enables a normal human being to do the impossible." - Marion C. Garretty

"There is no role in life that is more essential than that of motherhood." - Elder M. Russell Ballard

"God could not be everywhere, and therefore he made mothers." - Rudyard Kipling

"Being a mother is learning about strengths you didn't know you had." - Linda Wooten

"Mother—that was the bank where we deposited all our hurts and worries." - T. DeWitt Talmage

"A mother's love is everything. It is what brings a child into this world. It is what molds their entire being." - Unknown

"A mother is she who can take the place of all others but whose place no one else can take." - Cardinal Mermillod

"The mother's heart is
the child's schoolroom."
- Henry Ward Beecher

"No language can express the power and beauty and heroism of a mother's love." - Edwin Chapin

"A mother is the one who fills your heart in the first place." - Amy Tan

"Mother is one to whom you hurry when you are troubled." - Emily Dickinson

"My mother was my role model before I even knew what that word was." - Lisa Leslie

"To a child's ear, 'mother' is magic in any language." - Arlene Benedict

"A mother's love endures through all." - Washington Irving

"My mother is a walking miracle." - Leonardo DiCaprio

"A mother's hug lasts
long after she lets go."
- Unknown

"There is no way to be a perfect mother, and a million ways to be a good one." - Jill Churchill

"The natural state of motherhood is unselfishness." - Jessica Lange

"When you are looking at your mother, you are looking at the purest love you will ever know." - Charley Benetto

"Mother's love is infinite. A child can see it in her eyes, feel it in every hug, and hear it in every word of encouragement." - Unknown

"A mother's love is like a circle; it has no beginning and no ending." - Unknown

"In the mother's eyes, her smile, her stroking touch, the child reads the message: 'You are there!'" - Adrienne Rich

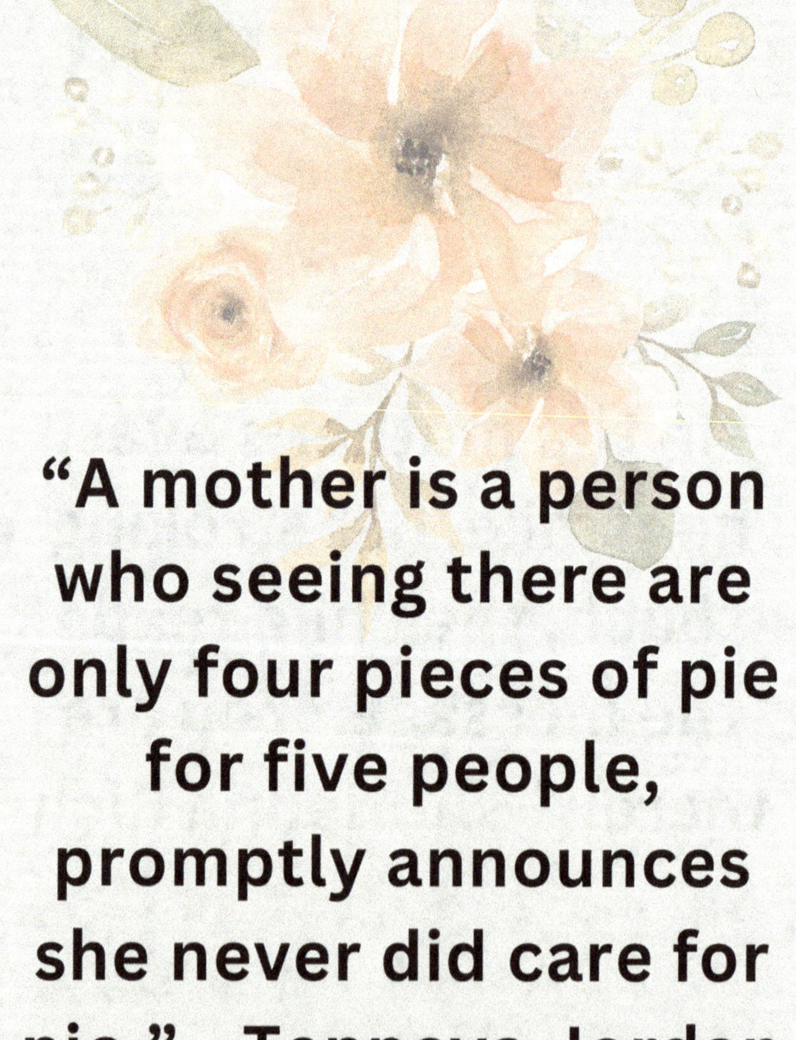

"A mother is a person who seeing there are only four pieces of pie for five people, promptly announces she never did care for pie." - Tenneva Jordan

"A mother's love is more beautiful than any fresh flower." - Debasish Mridha

"Mothers can look through a child's eyes and see tomorrow." - Reed Markham

"A mother is your first friend, your best friend, your forever friend." - Unknown

"The best medicine in the world is a mother's kiss." - Unknown

"A mother is always the beginning. She is how things begin." - Unknown

"We are born of love;
Love is our mother." -
Rumi

"Motherhood: It's not just a job. It's an adventure." - Unknown

"A mother's love is a grace that never judges." - Unknown

"A mother's love is a bond that connects us to the world." - Unknown

"A mother's love is the foundation upon which we build our lives." - Unknown

"A mother's love is a shelter from the storms of life." - Unknown

"A mother's love is a treasure that we carry with us always." - Unknown

"Whatever else is unsure in this stinking dunghill of a world a mother's love is not." - James Joyce

"The heart of a mother is a deep abyss at the bottom of which you will always find forgiveness." - Honore de Balzac

"Youth fades; love droops, the leaves of friendship fall; A mother's secret hope outlives them all." - Oliver Wendell Holmes

"A mother is the truest friend we have, when trials, heavy and sudden, fall upon us; when adversity takes the place of prosperity; when friends who rejoice with us in our sunshine, desert us when troubles thicken around us, still will she cling to us, and endeavor by her kind precepts and counsels to dissipate the clouds of darkness, and cause peace to return to our hearts." - Washington Irving